Vintage Spot Illustrations of Children

795 Cuts from the Teens and Twenties

Compiled and Arranged
by Judy M. Johnson

DOVER PUBLICATIONS, INC.
New York

Copyright © 1990 by Dover Publications, Inc.
All rights reserved under Pan American and International Copyright Conventions.

Published in Canada by General Publishing Company, Ltd., 30 Lesmill Road, Don Mills, Toronto, Ontario.
Published in the United Kingdom by Constable and Company, Ltd.

Vintage Spot Illustrations of Children: 795 Cuts from the Teens and Twenties is a new work, first published by Dover Publications, Inc., in 1990.

DOVER *Pictorial Archive* SERIES

Manufactured in the United States of America
Dover Publications, Inc., 31 East 2nd Street, Mineola, N.Y. 11501

Library of Congress Cataloging-in-Publication Data

Vintage spot illustrations of children : 795 cuts from the teens and
    twenties / compiled and arranged by Judy M. Johnson.
        p.   cm. — (Dover pictorial archive series)
    ISBN 0-486-26351-7 (pbk.)
    1. Children in art.   2. Illustration of books—20th century—
United States.   3. Magazine illustration—20th century—United
States.   I. Johnson, Judy M.   II. Series.
NC975.V5   1990
741.6′4′097309041—dc20   90-35482
                                                                              CIP

Introduction

SOME OF THE MOST delightful illustrations in American publications of the teens and twenties are those of children. These were the early days of magazines created just for children; at the same time, nearly every magazine of any kind that came into a family's home would have a special page just for the children, which would contain stories, games, paper dolls, paper toys, party ideas, crafts, fashions and more. Magazines for the lady of the house would have many articles about children, discussing health, discipline and diet, and would even contain stories about families. So there was ample opportunity for artists to render their conceptions of children of the day.

Holidays provided the basis for countless illustration ideas. Valentine's Day, with the making of valentines, was very popular; Easter chicks and bunnies gaily bounded into spring; Halloween brought with it exuberant antics, parties and spooky jack-o'-lanterns and witches; Thanksgiving was a time to reflect on the founding of this country; Christmas and New Year's were for family and church, with decorations, Santa, angels, trees, gifts and candles.

As children of these days did not have such diversions as television and school athletics, and there were rarely second cars for chauffeuring them to various activities, it was necessary for them to create their own entertainments. You will find dozens of these within the pages of this book: music, reading, winter recreation, playing with and caring for animals, arts and crafts, toys and games, dolls and just plain fun with one another. The child at home with mother and father provides the subject for some touching and charming illustrations. On the more prosaic side, we find children helping with household and farm chores, doing homework and going to school.

As for the fashions of the day, it hadn't been long since clothing began to be designed just for children. Up until the latter part of the nineteenth century, clothes for children were miniature versions of clothes for adults. But now children wore rompers and sunsuits and aprons and overalls and real play clothes that were distinctively childlike, and they were not only allowed to have fun but encouraged to do so. In the late teens we see some of the first differentiation of costume for boy and girl babies. Though even into the twenties boys still may be found in dresses up to the age of three (or until diapering was no longer required), a mother could also dress her little guy either in "unisex" fashions (they *never* would have said that word!) or in real little-boy styles, especially from about 1920 on. Little girls' fashions still maintained their delicate and pretty look, with ruffles and laces, buttons and bows, even when their mothers were wearing the boxy and plain styles of the Edwardian era and the simple, slimmer fashions of the early twenties.

We can scan the pictures of these days to gain a sense of style and pace, a sense of family and community that we may long to bring back. We can admire the technique and verve with which the artists rendered these scenes: the flow of line, the simplicity of form, the elegant composition, the whimsey, the accuracy in portraying the times. Or we can simply find pleasure in viewing fine representations of the life of children in the teens and twenties.

This book is dedicated to my mother, Helen, and my grandmother, Sylvia, for giving me the gift of a love of art, and for sharing old magazines for this collection.

JUDY M. JOHNSON

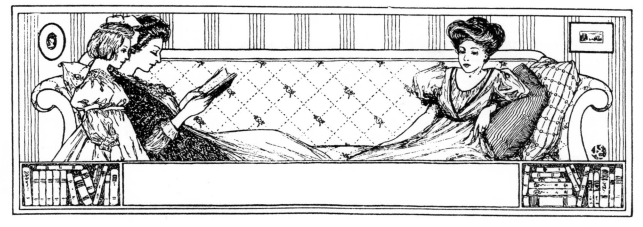

SCHOOL DAYS

CUT
OUT

CUT OUT

Margaret G. Hays

My chubby little nursery clock
Has a bright and jolly face;
It ticks so loud and fast and gay
You'd think it ran a race.
And all its chatter seems to be:
"You-can't-catch-me; you can't
catch-me."

JULIA HUSSANDER

1907

1907.

Violet Moore Higgins

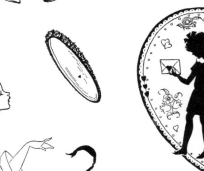

Playmates

Gangway!

Out Door Sports

Won't you be my Valentine?

TO MY VALENTINE

To my VALENTINE

MOTHER

I LOVE YOU

VALENTINE GREETINGS

EASTER
GREETING

Teepee

Thanksgiving

A CHRISTMAS LETTER
by Nancy Clinton

Dear (Santa), I thought I'd better write you just a little (letter) to tell you what we'd love to see all around our (tree). Ellen wants a baby— and a (house) and a (ball). Harry wants some (blocks) and oh, a 'lectric (train) that's sure to go; and a (drum) and (Indian) suit, and a (horn) for him to toot. John wants a (book) and (knife) and camping (stove) that really cooks. . . But please, I'd rather than all that have just a cuddly pussy—

A Merry Christmas

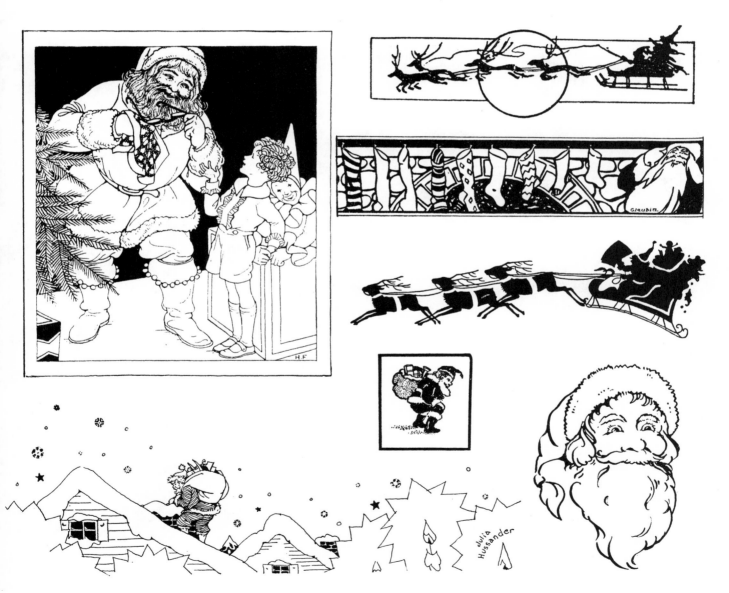

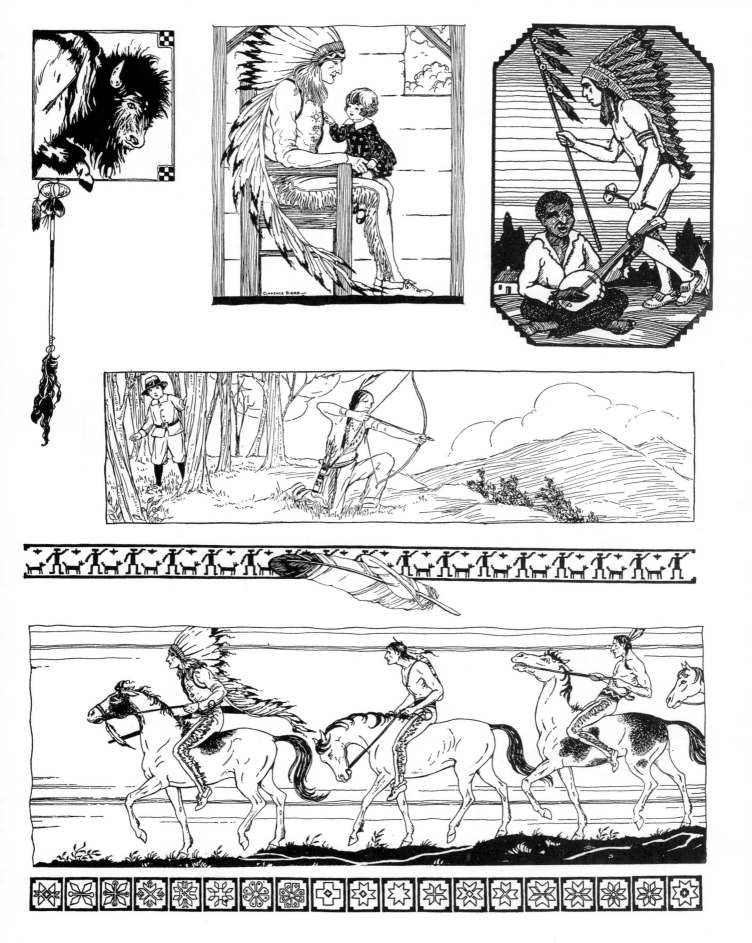

Cora
An Indian girl, Peru

Cut on dark lines

16th Century Costume

Girl's Hat.

Boy's Hat

Boy's Hat

Girl's Cap

ETHEL R. CLINE

JOHN BURES McKEE - 26.

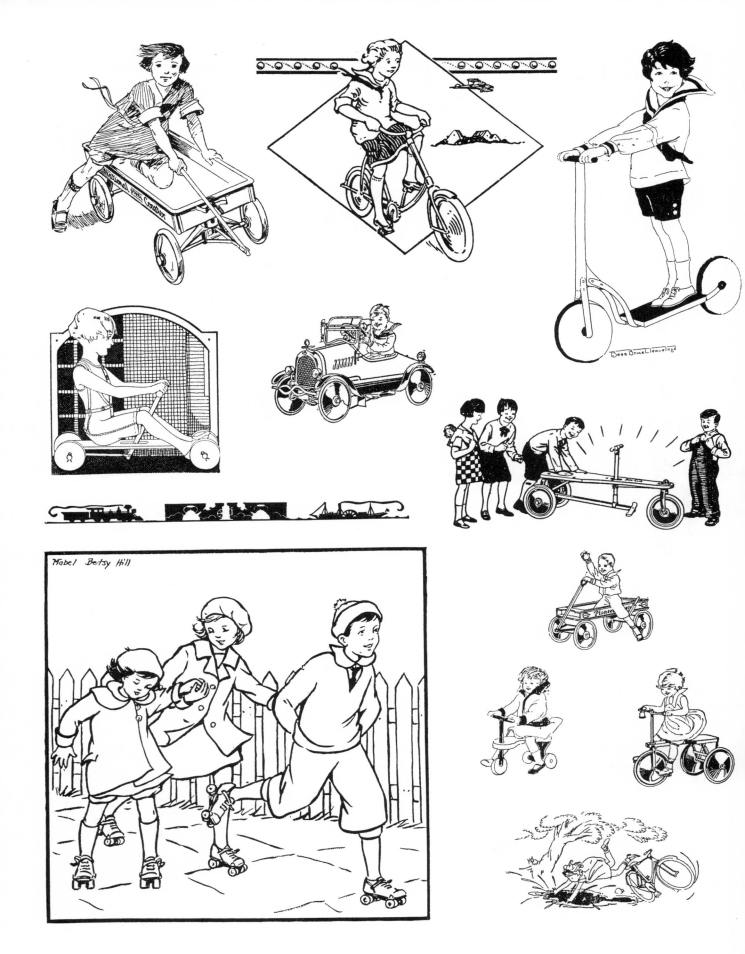

Squinkety-squank!
Squinkety-squank!

Ding! Dong! Bell!

Humpty-Dumpty

COW BOY

BOY BLUE

Toys and Games

DOG

SAILOR

CAT

FROG

CHICKEN

KEYSTONE
STEAM SHOVEL